Illustrated by Colorado Kids

RATTLESNAKE

Kate

Written by Natalie Myers

Colorado Kids Create, Inc. encourages artistic expression in youth and empowers Colorado teachers, raising funds for Art supplies.

Special thanks to Farra Larimore at Madwire, Danny Andjelkovich, Mark McFann, Bill Myers and Peggy Ford, Curator at the Greeley History Museum.
Thank you to cover artist, Melissa Lundy.

This book is for my daughters, sisters, and mothers, the bravest women I know.

Join in the fun of the annual, Colorado Kids Create drawing contest and win great prizes at:

coloradokidscreate.org

Purchase other Colorado Kids Create books on Amazon. CKC e-books are available on Kindle. Positive reviews are important so please leave one.
Reach us at coloradokidscreate@gmail.com

Have you ever seen a rattlesnake?

Once upon a fleeting time, in 1894, a little girl

was born in a log cabin in Northern Colorado.

Her name was Katherine Slaughterback.

Kate for short.

Kate grew up and had a son. Early one October

morning, she lifted 3-year-old, Ernie, onto her

4

saddle and the pair headed to a pond to hunt ducks.

As Kate hopped off her Pinto pony to open a gate

RaTTLe SSSSS RaTTLe

she heard a startling sound.

6

Rattle, rattle, sssss.

Rattle, rattle, sssss.

Rattle, rattle, ssss.

Grabbing a rifle, she saw that the snake wasn't

alone. Kate and Ernie were surrounded by snakes.

The slithering creatures were coming towards them.

It was a reptile migration!

What would you do

if this happened to you?

15

Kate's rifle was soon emptied of bullets.

She grabbed a fence post

16

and killed snake after snake.

The chain of reptiles seemed to

never end. After two hours,

140 rattlesnakes laid still

on the dusty earth.

The next day, Kate gathered the dead

snakes to skin and hang to dry.

Once the skins were tanned,

Kate made a dress, headband, and matching shoes.

With the largest rattles, she made a necklace.

She proudly wore her new apparel to a country

dance. How do you think she sounded?

Kate was a courageous woman of the West.

The late Bing Solomon wrote a song about her.

"Rattlesnake Kate was a legend, a lady of the

plains. Here's the story that stands behind how

Katie got her name. How Katie got her name. Now

Kate went out one morning, was on a sunny day.

Her boy sat right behind her as they rode along

their way, they rode along their way.

27

Out in the fields dismounted, she stopped right

in her tracks. A big, ole, angry rattlesnake

was buzzin' at her back,

he was buzzin' at her back.

(Chorus) Tune up the fiddle and rosin the bow,

Turkey in the Straw and Cotton-eyed Joe.

We'll have a time boys, don't you know

when Katie comes to town.

When Katie heard that buzzin', she looked down

at the ground, everywhere there were

32

rattlesnakes buzzin' all around,

buzzin' all around.

33

"Well, son, you stay up on that horse," was

all that lady said.

She shot a snake, grabbed some wood,

and started bashin' heads, started bashin' heads.

And when at last she stopped to rest,

her hands all bloody red,

lay all around her dead,

they lay all around her dead!

(Chorus) Tune up the fiddle and rosin the bow,

Turkey in the Straw and Cotton-eyed Joe.

39

We'll have a time boys, don't you know when

Katie comes to town.

Saturday night at a country dance,

excitements runnin' high.

We've waited for a month or more. There'll be a

dance tonight, there'll be a dance tonight.

Hands clap and fiddles ring, folks are steppin' high.

There's a jug at every fence post,

there's puddin', cake and pie,

There's puddin', cake and pie.

44

Then a hush falls on the crowd, what's this for

goodness sake? It's Katie dressed from head to

toe in the skin of rattlesnakes,

the skin of rattlesnakes.

(Chorus) Tune up the fiddle and rosin the bow,

Turkey in the Straw and Cotton-eyed Joe.

47

We'll have a time boys, don't you know,

when Katie comes to town."

Katherine Slaughterback's rattlesnake outfit can

be seen at the Greeley History Museum!

Thank You to the Following Colorado Kids!

Cover- Melissa Lundy, Delta Title Page- Claire Boyer, Windsor

Pg. 1. Nidhyat Jegadeesh, Fort Collins 2. Berit Larson, Lyons

3. Maya Saenz, Pueblo   4. Ava Oldenburg, Loveland

5. Cassidy Miller, Fort Collins 6. Sam Hoyt, Windsor

7. Aiden Dunbar, Windsor 8. Meredith Sauer, Windsor

9. Scarlett Storey, Milliken 10. Savannah Swift, Fort Collins

11. Monica Chacon, Greeley 12. Hans Meier, Peyton

13. Lucia Ramirex, Parker   14. Madison Murphy, Parker

15. Michael Elliot, Fort Collins   16. Jaelynn Leon, Peyton

17. Kait Heuer, Milliken   18. Laila Casanueva, Milliken

19. Eleanor Gillian, Fort Collins   20. Paiton Patterson, Windsor

21. Charlize Rodriguez, Pueblo 22. Alexia Rah, Windsor

23. Nora Myers, Evans   24. Sloan Speer, Steamboat Springs

25. Lily Burtis, Berthoud 26. Huy Lu, Denver

27. Adassah MacAlmon, Greeley 28. Rebecca Fairchild, Fort Collins

29. Ella Lee, Windsor   30. Abigail Towner, Pueblo

31. Abbie Winterbottom, Milliken, 32. A.J. Roth, Milliken

33. Andrea Ortiz, Fort Collins   34. Hannah Zhao, Denver

35. Felicity Tonnies, Fort Collins   36. Abigail Spencer, Peyton

37. Erin Chastain, Evans   38. Koen Hughes, Fort Collins

39. Adriana Rose, Parker   40. Andre Aparicio, Florence

41. Yunah Kim, Aurora 42. Devyn Luth, Windsor

43. Kate Ashenbrener, Parker   44. Kaden Taylor, Pueblo

45. Fenix Cervantes Quijano, Fort Collins 46. Cheyenne Turner, Windsor

47. Jordan Siples, Pueblo 48. Emilee McGuire, Windsor

49. Janey Mann, Milliken   51. Kearha Keith, Pueblo

Kill the snake of doubt in your soul crush the worms of fear in your heart and mountains will move out of your way. (Kristin Beachy)

RATTLESNAKE KATE
DAUGTER OF
WALLACE & ALBINA MCHALE
JULY 25, 1893 - OCT. 6, 1969

51

35347116R00031

Made in the USA
San Bernardino, CA
09 May 2019